C000184724

Pascal Vine is a UK performa
who enjoys describing the w
feeliest ways possible. He gra
Writing and Religion in 2018.
behind the scenes at many slams and open mics since starting
out five years ago, as well as headlined poetry nights across
the South West. He's worked with punks, interpretive dancers,
noise artists, radio hosts and anyone else who will let them. He
has been published by Bad Betty, Three Drops, and Verve in
various anthologies. He is disabled, nonbinary and tired.

Good Listeners

Pascal Vine

Burning Eye

BurningEyeBooks
Never Knowingly
Mainstream

This first edition published by Burning Eye Books 2022

www.burningeye.co.uk

@burningeyebooks

Burning Eye Books
15 West Hill, Portishead, BS20 6LG

ISBN 978-1-913958-20-6

Good Listeners

for myself

Contents

There are no vacancies

for someone to supervise the sun
as he lowers himself behind the hills.
Slowly, like he's got your father's
bad knees and ashy grimace.

And, this morning, I didn't need
to tell you that; clouds pass over
you like a chugger on a wide high street,
you're trying to tell them,
Look, you've got silver!

And they don't have the voice to ignore you,
or understand
that you can save the planet,
you have a vote that counts,
you contribute,
you can contribute.

I know the opening hours of your wounds,
the lights are still on inside you.
When you say you can't take
any more of this shit
you're stalling
to find new
huddled empties
we can call what is left of us.

Walking back from Unit 13

                                        Wrist-deep in a
                                    yesterday
                        fingers taut with it

            stuck like acrylic paint
                                    on the faded shirt
that you wear just to prove you did art
                        dig into an argument from years back

                        for an apology   to seep in
                        like rain in   soil
                                pollution on   everything

your mouth   surfaces first
            telling yourself to   stop

                welcome back   to paint flecks
            mizzle   part-time jobs

it is a cycle of pink   weeds
                    (*death-come-quickly*)
                rising from brickwork
                taught by the daylight

Pavement

for Shuggy & Sue

1. He gave me the mistakes with the hands he reserved for
   injured birds. I couldn't hear the words at first.
   It was okay; it was just drugs.
2. I didn't care what tattoos he had or how many faces he had
   to count before he went to sleep. I don't think he heard me;
   I don't think he could.
3. He always had tealights. He would listen for his name
   when I went walking at night. His soul could feel through
   the holes in his boots. It paid no mind that he made them
   and where he'd taken them.
4. Thank god he wasn't going to move for anyone; it was his
   street. (It still is.) If ghosts can walk through walls they can
   take up pavement and that is our problem.
5. I don't care if it wasn't enough; I knew him. He shook
   with courage. A sparrow-heart; a throng of regrets. He was
   made of little songs, a thousand sorrys roosting together to
   keep warm.
6. I will not flinch. I will not make way for an ending.
   There is time and kindness, and we are so abundant in
   each other. We should know what to do; we buried a loved
   man who thought he didn't deserve us.

A walk will help

Listen, for the

oh

is that it?

amongst the lush smithereens of March
in a nest of frothing lights
which are somehow towns
about ten miles off on the hills. If they
look back they won't see us. Night is disembowelled
into a work week. Jeremy Vine chirps
between the warehouses,
What does vermin even mean?
A fire front of rosehips and jackdaws
are closing in on grey puddles
on the concrete; they are blinked away
when they see me coming.
This is the closest apocalypse
available. A northbound 75 scavenges
through and I watch people watching us.
Everything glows on TV.
There are no natural predators here.

Arterial Road

the man is
Sick
i can   feel him
he's taken traces
of   my   fluorescence
with him   on the way
with no one

where i felt his shoes

he was on my back
so i know   he doesn't crawl
such good posture

i told him   he was the only one
to check on me
through the park
to the railings   on the   bridge
and   i told him

that i can watch the river
for him

there's so much room

Tone Vale

for Great Nanny Roscrow

I am sorry that they put you in a box.
I regret to inform you they did it again.

My mum played on the grounds of the asylum,
and then she huddled all the primroses

around your flat headstone. It's a quiet
place now, if that's what you want to hear.

Brick piles; gutted machines mid-snarl;
skylights tending nests of sparkling glass

beneath; a fuse box; the hiss of white walls.
People come because no one is there.

I am familiar with the ebb of bedrooms,
nurses and all kinds of punctuation.

I'll keep going,
if that's what you want to hear.

*Tone Vale hospital was established in 1892 in Taunton,
Somerset. A psychiatric hospital that is known to have pioneered
innovations in electroconvulsive therapy and transorbital
lobotomies. It closed in March 1995.*

All my friends were fucking sick

for Sunny

And they were all corpses
and they were all n/a
and they were all waiting

I wouldn't tell my children anything
I couldn't carry under my eyes
I will tell them to take these
noises & sympathies

and I would travel two hours
there and back to see my friends at
a noise show with white breath
in crap cafés past midnight
scuffing a concrete floor
wearing black shirts with black ink
crowding around the drums
like an animal we were trying to help

bobbing in the dark
showing one another
secrets we still had
like teeth
holding each other
like vigils

Moments.

I am in Waitrose, queuing because it's too far to walk to Lidl and because I want apple juice now, and I have just accidentally punched myself in the face because a loud noise happened.

Then it is six years ago, again. I'm flat on my back, staring up at a bone white ceiling; under the snarling and shivering I am buried.
Then I finally feel it, my face going from dry to wet. Dust settling. It hadn't rained in that hundred-year-silence until I learnt what a curse was and felt too heavy to lift it.

It's funny when it takes you, and your collarbone is crunching into your throat, shunting your headphones under your jaw, then your fist fills your eye socket in the space of a few barren seconds.
It is a landscape rearranging itself and something I was told to expect in another white room.

It is about thirty seconds until anyone speaks; I can't find the words for the moment as it took me, and my here-and-now body took it back.

I love it very much for that.

They can see me now. Sun-bleached, untouched, the calcified parts of me flaking away. I am in Waitrose, convincing the couple in front of me I'm okay. And they'll be fine; I think they needed to be told that. I just hit myself in the fucking face; what more could you want from your anecdote?
And then they get to leave.

I play my music again. Archaeology shifts awkwardly under my clothes. Everyone can see all the way down through my limestone and diatoms and glaciers. It must be fascinating.
My shoulders are chasms. They apologise. I apologise.

Breathe's apology

smoke seeps through
my coat as i walk through home
in the dark the air pregnant
with rain-smothered bonfires
now kicking in me because
i can't say no to an equinox.
crusted lips on mine
make a perfect black hole
i'd never even know was there
if i weren't looking up
the entire time. i'm thinking
about how contrails stick out
so much on may mornings
and that is what i decided to call
the lines on your skin
when you sleep naked and whether
i'll ever trust myself enough
to sleep naked again and i
also think about throwing up
in my mouth. poor boy.
he's wondering when it's gonna be
over and i'm still walking home
in the dark. i have his number
in my fist like it's the name of a
meteor that might one day kill
us all. i'm thinking about all
the syllables in his name
and how much they stick out
like exhaust fumes rehearsing
their words for the mist to make
a rainbow no one will ever see
i promise unless there are headlights.
i miss getting caught out.

Intervention

We had to gently explain to him
that he could already talk to ghosts.

Okay? he said, letting the delayed warmth
of our hands clip into each other. *Why?*

Because when he thought about life
it was lip-bitten, carbonated,

we saw him on the good days
when he didn't stop to think they were good days.

He nodded. *Yeah, they're in the distance
when I'm laughing, but they're not laughing.*

I said they know a different man
having a 4pm lie-in, bent like a black match,

morning-breath familiar. The dead only speak
one language, and you are well travelled.

Street

I check its pulse in the charity shops;
this town doesn't have a circulation
system, just a Spoons, a CEX and a
British Heart Foundation. I gave them
a duvet and three too-small shirts today; the lady
said they'd be perfect for a job interview.
I walk to the bus stop; I own the pavement
and the murals, now scabbed over. I'm in a queue with these
    blessings:

May you have the heart of an empty Sainsbury's
so you can have the courage to listen to your own
footsteps kick off the walls.

All the love in a Neil Diamond
song played for no one except you
and the people who are paid to be here.

May your veins be filled with day-old
flowers that will live to see the end of the week
for nothing.

I don't need to tell people
this is my hometown. You can hear the dust in the vowels.
Sunday hums a song without words behind to-let lips;
I see it smiling
through gutted Tesco under-eyes. The echoes have a sesh
in underfunded libraries fuelled by volunteers,

those old ladies who keep this town bleeding.
You can see where you are in the dark windows;
don't let them tell you you're nowhere.

It was natural to run.

I'm not being killed;
I'm my own verb right now.

A kigo.
Mangled. Popped.
Midnight.

You are not hearing
a baby cry for its mother. That's me,
April.

I will glisten
an unhinged crimson
and the fox will drag
me and make moon-roads
in the dew

as I am amputated
from this world.

As much as it is
what mothers do,
it is what we rabbits sing;

bury me one last time.

Beltaine

Let me in.

I'm trying to shove my eyes back
            into their sockets with their lids;
my knuckles are an   inside colour
        from climbing trees,
my jaw is tight
and this religion is heavy.

                        I haven't made   anything today.
            Let me in.

I look up
                    the sunbeams   through   the green
split.
        I am stuck, there is raw voice in the canopy,

        Let   me be a habitat.

        the wind caves in on me
and I am   probably going to hell.

        I shut myself back into this skull
        like I will fit this   time
and I haven't lost my keys,

        as if I am not too wide and two legs
and a strange pulping   muscle
        keeping time with my mistakes.

        Let me in,
        I need to breathe through my fingers,
I need to die slower.
Please. Let me in.

It isn't the jay cry that brings
me out; it's the *if, but, yet*
of the mud. That, and the hum of miles in my feet
through holey socks.

I find the syllable somewhere in me: home.
I don't even knock any more.

The path of most resistance

A hip socket that spits like a green log
in a new fire. Knuckles that sympathise
with a frustration of grass snapped in the frost;
this is all we need to speak
with the land. The yew bough that squeaks
over grave plots,
the rock that tics in the river bed,
and the storm's stims have been told
they're good listeners.
Now sing.

Hummingbird Hawk Moth

for Ma

Jesus feels like an insect
I am trying to set free
from the church.
But for now, I am holding
him as he clambers in the dark
space of my unwashed palms. *Forgive me,*
I'm taking you
where you belong.
I open my hands
in the graveyard. His calling
is bare. The lime trees
scalped and wretched
with trying flowers.
His wings billow in place; I see fire,
briefly, and something human.

Celandines

A grandparent is someone who teaches you to die
behind closed doors,

who gives you a name that means beautiful-don't-touch
in the hedgerow-tongue.

She gave me anxiety and living things.

When I close my eyes
I'm overgrown,
I'm crawling,
I'm the weevil grub oozing out the green acorn.

I name everything to find myself;

celandines screw up like little yellow arseholes
when the air pressure drops;
catkin willow boughs scrawl like GP prescriptions;
hawthorns have a death-smell;
people have a death-smell.

She taught me that
you can look like a bird
and that can be a bad thing.

That you don't have to sleep,
or eat, when you're not here,

that grace is not a virtue
when it is dry-swallowed by your last days.

That you don't mean

the frost crunch of phlegmed coughs,
snowfall into specimen cups,

this season of lying down
for the last time. You mean

beautiful,

don't touch.

My Lady

The first thing they teach you
is that she lives in everything;

willow hunched into crutches
and stair rails,
dog rose blossom
collapsing as soon as it opens,
and still water in deep, gouged channels.

A crooked hand was here;
crumpled goddess forms
in an orthopaedic landscape;
there is a truth having a depression nap
under your unproductive feet.

The second thing you learn
yourself; the natural conclusion.

I hope I'm warm. I hope she is
snug under my subluxes
as she creaks psalms
for mutual safe passage.

Take your boneknit and honey;
she knows what's good for us.

The third thing is that you can
never call her useless again.

A country

He tells you he has three months of citalopram spare, if you need it. I make a wish on him, he is bright, he is above you and he might not come back.

I only talk to strangers when it is necessary, you lie. Your prayers are getting dusty, you don't have time for hobbies. Your neighbours don't know your new name; you come to church for the cake and bodies. Your friends are in cities.

I am in a kind of city; when you lie in bed there's foot traffic. Your thoughts are shortcuts. Answers roar like tyres through rain. They pool together again, and you accept that you'll never see the bottom of them.
You go to sleep, again.

You dream. *There is a home. Wind in trees and grey sky beaches. Plaques on benches. Chats with men in Big Issue jackets. Starlings spasming at the end of summer, tides of stars breaking over autumn clouds. Well-lit streets. Babies on buses. Fluttering libraries. Open mics. Pub hum. Carnival. Cider. Blackbirds. Good intentions.*

It must feel like home; something has to feel like that trick of the light, and then you look directly at it, it beckons to you through the phosphenes.

Dead friends, deader strangers.
Sleeping bags.
Years pass. Moon phases. Eating themselves until someone somewhere must be full.
I reach out, smudged and clingy, read my stained fingers,

'a loneliness – of
immigrants – swarm – our promises.'

You wake up, *dark and satanic.*
You make a precious decision and start walking.

Slept in eyeliner mist at the train station; everything is vein-coloured and close. Perfect day to go missing. Let the land make a trust fall as I pass. Curl up into an anthem on an empty seat. I am done with islands. Leave behind the only compromise I've ever known.

Let someone inspect you, find that you are full of holepunches the light has escaped through.

You will shine whether you like it or not.

Acknowledgements

I want to sincerely thank everyone who made this pamphlet possible, for helping me create something that cannot be taken away from me. Bridget Hart, Clive Birnie and Harriet Evans have been excellent for their support, hard work and patience.

Many people looked over this work before it came to light, including the important feedback of audiences and wonderful fellow poets at open mic poetry nights and gigs. Thank you to those who have workshopped and looked over these poems in the last two years; Sam Grudgings, Saili Katebe, Oska Von Ruhland, Tom Sastry, Callum Wensley, Moss Rumboldt, Alex Calver and the wonderful Emma. Thank you to the effervecent team at Tonic Bristol who decided to give me a chance and grow my confidence, Taran Spalding-Jenkin and Chris Beale. Thank you to Malaika Kegode and Rebecca Tantony for providing mentoring and guidance as well as very touching words. And finally, Rhys Ashton Tucker is a miracle and has doggedly supported me every step of the way.

Thank you to my sister, Lucie, for being a wild, lovely and perfect sister who was always happy to look over my writing. Thank you to my Dad who has constantly put up with my antics and nonsense, and starred as the unflattering opening line to this pamphlet. Thank you to my Ma, who has always been there to cringe and clap through the best and the worst of my work from the beginning.

Thank you, person reading this, for doing the whole reading malarkey.

Lightning Source UK Ltd.
Milton Keynes UK
UKHW021316020922
408223UK00006B/502